The Temporary World

Poems by

Martin Willitts Jr.

BLUE LIGHT PRESS ❖ 1ST WORLD PUBLISHING

1ST WORLD
PUBLISHING

SAN FRANCISCO ❖ FAIRFIELD ❖ DELHI

Winner of the 2019 Blue Light Book Award
The Temporary World
Copyright ©2019 by Martin Willitts Jr.

1st World Library
PO Box 2211
Fairfield, IA 52556
www.1stworldpublishing.com

Blue Light Press
www.bluelightpress.com
bluelightpress@aol.com

Book & Cover Photo & Design
Melanie Gendron
melaniegendron999@gmail.com

Author Photo
Linda Griggs

First Edition

Library of Congress Control Number: 2019946838

ISBN 9781421836348

The Temporary World

Table of Contents

I. Before

II. During

III. After

Dedicated to my wife, Linda Griggs

I. Before

Before Words

1.

Before words, days had no meaning.
We could draw antelopes leaping energy off cliffs.

We could go in any direction because no boundaries existed.
Yellow mustard days were within reach.

There was no reason to want anything
in the dawning of words.

2.

Somebody wanted more —

more flint; more ripe raspberries;
more land someone else had —

to get more, they forged words
for hunting or berries
or bad weather or danger.

3.

Language was created
when a man carved a naked woman
with enlarged breasts
on a mastodon's ivory
and still had no words
to express his feelings.

Even when he owned words,
he never could explain his feelings
any more than he could rip the moon
out of the midnight sky
or stop that emptying feeling in his heart.

So, when a woman walked away,
her breasts swaying,
it left him wondering
what he should have said,

how comforting were those breasts
whenever he snuggled against them,
how her face in the moonlight calmed him,
how her body was smooth as the bone
he was carving —

stroking the memory-idol of her body,
reclaiming the calm of turtle-wind.

4.

Language was created
when a woman gave birth,
pushing a child out
of the cave of her body —

a baby swimming out
into the waiting hands
of a female shaman
fingering an amulet of bloodstone
evoking visions
to name the child.

5.

Men conspired then
to own all of the mysteries,

hunting the night for answers,
naming the sun, a male god.

6.

God tossed out words
from his velvet mouth:

raindrops

men caught them all.

Before Letters

1.

Before eels swam in electric water,
before words were written,
a man walked in the Alps,
wearing deerskin boots,
searching for missing sheep
in wind howling like hungry wolves.

A sudden avalanche took him and his screams away.

2.

When someone found the frozen, ancient body.
thousands of centuries later,
it looked as if he had been trying to write something
with the sewing needle
used to mend his handmade boots.

3.

Words roam loose —
fitting all descriptions,
escaping boundaries of this page,
taking the odor of printing presses
and the touch of laughter.

4.

Words are unruly, disobedient,
sticking their tongues out.

Words gather as a distrustful crowd,
following us down gloomy passageways.

Our hearts are loud and struggling,
but words do not want to listen.

Words pick out meaning
as the nocturnal insect of death.

Before Music

1.

Before music, there was no sound.
The universe was speechless —
an un-plucked harp
defiant in the void,
not hearing the wake-up call,
setting creation
in constant motion.

Before then, there was nothing,
and no one was listening.

2.

On a white-hot night,
you could hear the rumble of heat

like folding chairs snapping,
body oozing quarter notes,

no breeze, uncomfortable blasts
full of Jazz flames,

explosions of new suns,
rustling of anger,

clash of cymbals,
then creation was exhausted.

You could almost smell fresh wet clay.
This was how life began.

3.

There is no sweeter sound
than two lovers stroking as violins,
or a baby's trombone cry.

Before music,
silence was an empty cathedral
and chaos was parched trees.

4.

When a woman heard a man's heartbeat,
terrified of his own darkness,
she invented a drum to capture it.

When a man heard a woman's softness
coaxing strawberries into tasting like love,
he fluted stars to whirl around her halo.

The music of life, began,
a chorus of hope in laughter.

5.

I pour water over my frenzied body
trying to cool my body temperature.
No sleep is in the forecast.
I am restless as a piccolo,
disturbed as Amadeus,
distant as the stilled wind,
sudden as the embarrassed applause,
gone as music escaping the ear.

6.

Anxiety jitterbugs
at dissatisfied dance floors,
language twirls with skirts flying,
bobby socks white as expectation,
flashing legs of misunderstandings.

We pick up conversations,
asking for names
in the swirl of dance floors partners.

The continued swaying,
mating rituals are always this frantic,
the crude introductions, then
slow-dancing through assurances

or fast dancing to intimacy.

7.

When the band stops playing,
the final note held delicately
between interconnected hands
with a hint of music in the soft kiss,
our minds hold a filled dance card,
a wild card of tomorrows,
a tarot card of the *Fool in Love*
wearing awkward ballet slippers
ready to swan-leap
into the orchestra pit of love
or into the twisted tubas of divorce.

8.

There is a black hole in our hearts
where the music should be.
Dark birds migrate into our faces,
lifting the night canvas,
but our hearts should not be starless.

The universe is alive with secret language.

Before Drama and Dance

1.

vibrating between worlds
a shaman put on a deer skull

painting his face with pokeberries
slicked hair back with bear grease

until at last
we had understanding

2.

we are not allowed to see his face twisted
in the False Face Society

or long-beak raven
or burial mask

for to know the real person
is to invite colliding worlds

our ancestors
would tumble into the void

3.

before religion
there were storytellers

before the dance of lies
the mask of words

Before Numbers

1.

before numbers
the world was within sight
we could walk to the border
and there was no edge
marking beginning or end

we never knew how far
or close we were to disaster

never knew heights or depths
never knew our limits

numbers changed the calculations

2.

the world was simpler then
you traded objects

a man could build his own house
with rough hands
and measure with his feet

anything more
or less
anywhere further beyond walking
beyond sight
was beyond wanting

3.

someone decided standard numbers
were necessary to know
how many or how few or
how much or how little
or how they lived without numbers

someone wanted imaginary numbers
someone wanted more
someone was counting on it

4.

after numbers were assigned
man discovered he really did not want
the number of problems

and even zero
had value

5.

a pyramid of decimals greets me at the door
fractions ride barrels over Niagara Falls
clouds practice long-division, problems multiply
algebra is as seasonal as blueberries
gravity plops newspapers to my doorstep
a whirlwind of minus signs darkens
the vanishing-point sky
numbers are juggled by accountants

6.

one is an open door

two is a Blues number playing
when your lover is a two-timer

the grocery store scales are weightless
until filled
by three artichokes at the counter

four lost letters arrive
they do not belong to me
they do not belong to this address
I break them open like eggs

five wooly mammoths trumpet loudly
their wet fur stinks of tundra
they buy electric shavers
and breath mints
they pay with six gold doubloons

7.

on my seventeenth year
a 65 cherry-red Chevy pulls up
taking me past my 11 o'clock curfew
burning all four rubbers

if you gave me ten rules
I'd break them into 57 pieces

gravity cannot hold a teenager
that has any number of excuses
and a fake ID

8.

now age limits me
miles abuse my face
gravity keeps me nine to five
a regular guy
listing rules
for my teenage son
knowing full well
he'll break them all
plus some extra ones
like a combination lock

I can count on it

Before Drawing

1.

before there were visions
dawn was colorless and damp

night was a tar pit of primal confusion
no one played harmonic blue notes
the palette emptied of colors

men gathered in caves
during snow
endlessly waiting in harsh grey conditions

fire was created
by accidental lightning

someone left a bloody handprint on a cave wall

then everything fell into place
like dominos

someone drew conclusions
stylized bison leapt out
shadowed by possessed hunters

and the end of everything

2.

we have forgotten how to mix paint with eggs

simple structures like oranges
are not round

wars were won by the best mapmakers

we celebrated imperfect nudes
until we wore colorful fabric

3.

after we trapped rainbows into paint
desperation was green-sighing

no two vanishing points meeting
until someone steps back
becoming lost in the moment

4.

on the eighth day
god created communication
and man forgot
to write it down

man tried to blame his hazy mind
after seeing the sharp burgundy
of a woman's fresh nipples
his feet melting into clay

teeth chattering nonsense
trying to impress her and failing
his hands carving his feelings on stone

no wonder creation is in every story

Before Tools

1.

Before man could handle tools,
he hid up in trees.

Once he discovered a rock could smash,
his slow brain finally opened

to spears to bows and arrows
to gun fire to nuclear bombs.

2.

Before, tree branches had to fall
or a diseased tree would have to topple,

but once man noticed beavers gnawing on trees,
he invented saws:

the jagged-teeth evident as a smirk.
All he needed was an ax to grind.

3.

Not all simple machines are simple designs.
Cams and gears take two parts to move,
and sometimes need a leather belt to turn a motor.
If gears slip, it is as dangerous
as any argument where no one wins.

4.

A woman must have seen a borer beetle
when she invented the screw.
When man did not know what to do with that,
she created the screwdriver,

so, naturally, man thought it was a sex object.

Woman knew a dim bulb when she saw one.
She designed the lightbulb,
but man was still in the dark.

II. During

Entering

It occurs to me:
coming to myself

as a stranger,
entering into *Other* space

the edge of a *verge* is something to like.
Choices do not have to be complete to be *there*.

Dredging a river does not remove everything,
let alone expose our search.

Is there enough *emptying* before *nothing* is left?

Letter

A half-mad letter was in my pocket all day
reminding me
things were not going well.
Not at all.

In the amount of removed light,
it sent distraught messages
no one wanted to hear.

Its letters were moving around in my pocket,
exploring
how things should always be good,
but they never are.

I wanted the blueprint of memories.

Glass

1.

People were removing glass from their eyes.
They looked to the side through broken wings.
There were no waves on the curve of light.

2.

If we open windows of memory,
we will notice they were nailed shut.

We can put our hands, delicately, through empty panes.

Choices

earth clenches fiercely
whatever heat it has left
crackling
filing grievances
holding back
its music box
of birds
at a safe distance

there is a large book of questions
opened less than when we were young

a rickety door opens other possibilities

enter

A Red Box

A visitor brings mystery — a red box
without a secure lock. *Don't open;
let it happen.*

There are voices inside,
demands none of us meet.
Insistence makes curious noises.

There are things we hear
when nothing is spoken.
There are strangers inside me,

not ignoring judgment,
not considering: *Let it happen.*

Differences pronounce sameness;
almost transferable.

Someone overlaid words like un-mortared bricks.

Language Finds Its Way

Once we begin noticing, our eyes
cannot get enough of every detail:
a blue tint on black crow feathers;
a fence post wood grain wavering;

or light between a tern's wings
softened by cool air; or buttercups
making yellow laughter; or silt
edging into water when it ebbs;

or the first four seconds
when a baby breathes.
Language finds its way towards the unspoken.
All loss falls apart.

Depleted Uranium

I am what happens when things flow wrong.
I am what does not go away.
I contaminate prayers with sorrow.
I am what never ends when you want it termination.
I am things out of control.
I am one of those problems
increasing exponentially. The only certainty
is uncertainty. This is what it looks like
to be half-life.

Robert Rauschenberg's "*Canyon*"

1959

Assemble house paint onto sky.
Pencil in despair, like slow-moving hooves
tearing the paper canyons.

This fabric is sharpened by talons, metal
in the eyegleam, when oil rigs
are cactus peyote button hallucinations.

Nail me to the cardboard sunrise;
I am not here anymore.

Poetry or photographs cannot explain
what mirages can:

wood solid as paint tubes;
pillow clouds and bald eagle
ripping images into sinew,
fleshmeat, boned:
parts of the whole; parts leaving a hole —
all fragments, impaired dreams.

Ask me again what I think.
I might have another answer.

Untitled

only a few house lights remain
cold darkening

houses disappear
shimmering loss

reluctant breath making small clouds
light pulled inside

A Rawness We Do Not Understand

Based on the painting, *"The Raft of the Medusa,"*
Théodore Géricault, 1819

This condemned raft on doomed waves
is paralyzing dark. Some cling,
some sing, some curse to no avail. Rudderless
sea birds not knowing the *somewhere land.*
Some lash with what they can, feeble, thirst-
drained in salt water, hallucinating.
Emptiness is sobbing. Some die, some slip away,
some cannibalize the dying while they are alive. It edits.
There is no resolve. No resolution. The ocean is dark-red;
the sky is a purple bruise. Some cry *mercy*
where there is none. The raft has no choice.
It tosses what it does not need into the gone.
We draw lots to see who is next. Thirst baptizes us.
The few become less. Survival eats at what remains.
The storm is a cannibal of relief. Another slips over.
How fatal we are when first we begin to pretend.

During a Conversation of Many Voices

Some were carried undertow
into a drowning.
The distant shore was elusive.

Some were taken away — stiff currents;
lightning striking water,
churning them into blood.
Still no one noticed.

The roar was overcoming. Seagulls flew out
of the harbors of our arms,
still
no one noticed the floundering.

Out of the drenching,
wearing slickers,
waving lanterns, no shore in sight,
no one noticed
how everyone's mouths
opened, closed,
like fish on land.

I kept the oars to myself.

Only dark clouds opened their hands
and let go.

Fishing Before Dawn

steam rises off a mourning lake
mist stirs resemblance
the sky falls into my lap

I begin speaking to the dying

Lifting Out of Ourselves

1.

We all have a fervent wish
to lift out of our bones into a sublime sky
shedding skin —

then, deepness impenetrable.

Within split milliseconds,
sunken silence
empties the bowl of itself.

2.

There is a lifeline map in our palms,
disturbance of belief beyond singular breath,
in which everything snaps into place,
opens its segments to reveal
a shining, intangible formula
of augmented line.

3.

Nature is impartial. No judgment,
no finger-pointing, no forbidding,
no condensation of breath into tropical birds,
no revision of light. Only the return —

the giving endlessly of love —
branches of elevated love in absolved light.

4.

Rugged land, rubbed smooth
by a carpenter's plane, sandpaper fine —
solitudes of cold streams
find memory:

lopsided furrows of plowed ages,
daybreak-ecstasy dew:

enough to break a heart into twigs.

5.

Changeable weather
beyond awakening, untangling.
Gravity loses its hold.

6.

The nimblest, smallest object:
a careful, invisible hand;
feathers of rain; stillness passing,
leaving everyone behind.

Touch

Touch is the willingness to be vulnerable,
Sometimes a weighted risk
a cost-accountant tally on a ledger.

Being vulnerable is opening musty drawers.
You have to enter into the unknown,
stepping onto loose stones in a stream,
hoping the stones will not tilt.

What you do will affect what happens next.
Tug too hard on blinds, they crash.
Light blasts in, the world loses shape,
vanishes.

Focusing Past Loss

I'm reminded at the most inopportune moments,
I've outlived my critics. I remember, running
in blistering sun, then laying in grass, focusing
on one blade, until it blurred, seeing through it,
seeing chlorophyll moving, risking
weightlessness, leaving my body behind.
I was tending to the needs of loss, mothering,
breaking free of cell membrane.

What We Do Not Know

When the disappearing
reappear,

Others
swirl from below.

What speaks?
What whispers?
Birds of cold reckoning.

What was invisible
is not hidden
anymore —

voices
in the held-back silence —

a rapture of birds
released
after a long flood.

III. After

Ownership

Morning released vocabulary
into the unwelcoming world.

When words arrived at their destination,
they were misunderstood.

A basket with colored light
lasts only as long as sunlight fills it.

Silence

switch on the moon
crickets serenade

ambient light tells me
we are still alive
not dreaming
all of this

termites
stop nibbling at the flesh of this house
a rough crescendo

Air

I could not tell you then how close you were to death,
blue as a stone,
how chickadees stopped their tormenting love long enough
to feel pity, how silence sat in a rocking chair, holding the pulse
of a blue vein, looking for some faint sigh of light.
I could not tell you then, for I needed you to fight back,
my rescue breathing had failed.

I cracked your ribs like walnut shells, forcing space to push out
the Nothingness inhabiting you, section by section, occupying
what should be, by rights, yours.

I could not tell you over the coldness,
the shifting iceberg in your bones, that I was losing you.
You had to find your own way back.

I waved frantically, *this way*.
I could not tell you, because you could not hear.

You were not here. You were headed to the Elsewhere.
My training was failing both of us; and you were heading
towards that more insistent calling. All I was holding
was the stone of your life.

They told me I had done everything. I had been at it for hours.
I worked while you were dead. This was no comfort.
I saw you in the blue moon, the unmoving rocking chair,
the air you never had, the coldness of summer at noon,
bones cracking like ribs, the light on a walnut shell.

Flight

In hollow bones is flight-memory —
primeval rivers they've followed,
intersections of dream-weavings

through changeling sky, dark with stars,

fused breastbone to support wings
that span where we cannot see,

migrating the same territory to know
what is over the curve of the horizon,

navigating and exploring,

nesting,
re-telling songs of flying:

flirt, dash, dart,
loop, wind current, air draft, lift —

musical notes, heartbeats,

narrowing vision,
focused only on the familiar:

the hover; the feeder.

Urge circumnavigates
infinite possibilities.

Walking into Remembrance

1.

My life was a waning moon, where belief comes and goes.

Sounds of waterfalls change.
Clouds are eternal islands always transforming.
Why not me?

Heavy dew-fall of plums; a shadow at noon,
a distance where the missing are more interesting
than the found.

2.

A garden without a coat, shivers loose feeding birds.
Birds are erased and reappear, but with new colors.

Stars spill out of chrysanthemums as if from jars.
Clouds are burning in exhausted shade.

The world is in turmoil thinking you might be gone someday.
Don't walk so far into memory you can't come back.

Omen

a vortex of birds
waking sky
splitting clouds
exposing excitable light

they take off
springing flashes
color and sound

violins tuning
before a great classical performance
one piccolo
heard above the register

In Between

Before your heart blinks out,
wind must shed cherry petals.

It hesitates. It plunges into the unknown
where we all must go.

The sky closes shutters, but some light comes through.
There is the smell of *Always*.

A mountain laments — fog.
A hand tugs at birds.

Before you left, you were here,
and Nothing listened —

Nothing was a pond of light.
Light though pinfeathers.

A rustle of air against air.
Many moons in many raindrops.

Before *before* there was
Nothing.

The absence loudly proclaiming its silence.

Glass Walls Do Not a Barrier Make

Based on *Open Box 3,* by Joel Haber

Put a glass wall to hide the truth; you can still see it.
Tear out the windows like black eyes, empty our sockets;
we are not blind to our situation.
Prop up the sides of our house and declare it safe;
it will fall on us with the next light wind.
Chain the glass to poles, thinking it will stop winds;
the winds will simply cross over and topple us.

The island can rise up into the air, but it takes more
to help an island to repair itself, takes more
for people to pick up the splinters. Open a box,
and misery will go with the winds, perhaps, to you,
and if you wake up devastated, you will understand.

If you want to do something useful, do it quickly.
Otherwise, do not pretend my house is invisible,
when it is clearly behind a glass wall.
Do not pretend my house has chairs and walls,
do not mistake the broken wood scattered everywhere
as edible or practical for repairs.

Certainly, do not think this is just a diorama
representing the worse of conditions.
Our lives are torn, blackened refugees.

As the wind goes, so too the sand.

Not Seeing Eye-to-Eye

Not seeing eye-to-eye, avoiding seeing
what is in front of us, when all we could see
was clear sailing. There is no boat in this story.
No oars to cling to. Only drowning.

Not looking into the other's eyes is a sign
of avoiding the obvious. What were we supposed to see?
The sign should have said: *Danger ahead*.
But we cruised as if the roads were speedways.

We ignored the turnoffs. We thought we knew
where we were going, and it did not matter
how we get there. We forgot to go together.
We could blame the maps. I could.

Now you are somewhere else. I got lost on my own.
I found another traveling companion.
When I looked into her eyes, she was not hitchhiking.

Weightless as Blossoms in Wind

in a field of white lit lanterns
petals fall like white moths
taking fragrance with them

the amazing is always on the other side of the door
all you need to do is pry it open and peer inside

Not Exactly Sleight-of-Hand

I trace the blue vein
to your breasts

when I do
sparks emit from your body
two crossed unlike wires

causing edges of snow
beyond corruptible light

· · ·

disappearing weightlessly
into tree bark
was the easiest thing
I had ever done

turning into rice paper
for plum ink
was more challenging

Prelude to Death

What rises —
fog, steam, or laughter?
A sonata
from Bach's hand
arriving
at the right pitch
of silence,
sheet music
you could climb like ladders
to heaven
gathering notes like jays,
ascending amazing space
saying,
I want this!

Rain is the Face of Desolation

1.

the rain lacks imagination
falling wherever without thinking
unconsciously of cause and effect

the size of the rain is random
it could last several days
the results would still be the same

what causes more concern
is the lack of rain

2.

when weather has no destination
each day is unending

weather is trying many different aspects
of misery to see which one fits best

sometimes it is the surface of silence
small as a pinch of salt.

sometimes it is knocking on a door
no one answers

sometimes crows discuss the weather
as a source of all blackness

3.

rain pings against my window
white shavings of crane feathers
like monks sweeping drops of silence

those monks are not monks
but cranes attaching torn paper napkins to clouds
footprints of rain on a long journey

rain lingers
a rejected lover

4.

monsoons wrinkle on my face
drenching everything in sight
until it is hard to see

the sky empties its belly

only the water spider can walk in this
and then slowly with extreme care

5.

what is transparent
hides what is underneath

Some days

I can imagine the world without me.
It troubles me, this knowledge,
the truth of what it means.

For the certainty of days
and the certainty of nights,
there are continuous moments.

Sometimes, I imagine you without me —
and that too troubles me — so much time lost between us,
so many times, when we could have said one last goodbye.

How, too, I think, endlessly,
the heart continues
and somehow it mends itself.

If there is comfort in this, let it remain.
If it troubles you, let it go.

Nocturne

Let snow fall — paper cutout flakes.
Let the ebony moon wander in its tiny apartment.
Let flammable birds exit your name.
When you die, bulrushes will weep constellations.

In the nave of a church, mourners hide purple shrouds.
In polished wooden pews,
grief is eighty-six black and white piano keys.
The instrument of sadness is only one note.

In a tree is hidden firelight.
From the smallest oleander, a hummingbird extracts love.
Grief is such a tiny box until you open its contents.
When you die, a new island will be created.

Is There a Beyond?

Ashes are the beginning and omega.
First, kindle fire; then, when wood burns down,
the cycle repeats. Is ash new or old life?
Is there a Beyond *beyond* the Beyond?

Yes, sizzle the cicadas, *like snowflakes*,
belonging and not belonging, sharing strangeness.
Soundless branches know distance and closeness,
both being in sunlight and darkness —
shells of wrinkling voices; all disappearances.

How Objects Take on New Meanings

he sees her empty chair
absence takes another meaning

she is his next thought
trying to fill the missing

blackened edges of grief
heart removing words

a blue jay squawks
warning she's dying

when he is asleep
she watches his loss already forming

The Unexplained Explained

We don't have language
to explain loss to each other.
Words hijack meaning.

All abandoned languages
are chipped, porcelain teacups
with fake gold trim around the lip.

We have seen repercussions of a pebble
dropped into water, the aftereffect
when stone inhabits the *Unknown*,
consumed in thoroughly darkening light.

The *Other*

I looked over and saw the *Other*,
and the *Other* did not look like me,
did not sound like me.
There was no comfort in that thought.

A maelstrom of faces appeared
all speaking a confluence of languages.

If I should not change the *Other*
and the *Other* should not change me,
then why am I disturbed?

A voiceless silence answers

Improvisations in Darkness

1.

The delineation from lamp,
circuitous
around a corner, into
a dark room, narrowing
into lost light,
disappearing —
one reality
into another.

Going into the unknown,
expect surprises.

2.

Going from dark
into darker,
there is always
ambient light —

rain
against windows:
soft, hard,
then noticing

it's gone.

3.

In Total Darkness,
you develop a sense
of where things are.

You do not need to see them.
You know their shape,
density, their dark purpose,
knowing how to avoid them
using radar.

If only
this worked in relationships,
there would be no failure,

we'd all know what to do,
who to avoid,
what to say, when to say it
instead of blurting
the first thing
coming to the tip of our tongue
with no way
to reel it back in.

4.

In Total Darkness
there is no such thing
as darkness.

The lack of light,
is the lack of imagination.

True blindness
is not seeing things
for themselves.

We do this in first love.

Light comes on.
We realize we made a mistake,
an error in judgment,
darkness floods our hearts,
switches off our brains,
drains blood from our veins.

Blindness continues
even after knowing the facts.

5.

In Total Darkness
we learn to use other senses,
the ones less traveled —

pinpricks of awareness,
air against skin,

hair on our arms, rising
like antennas.

Emerge into light
with the same, tentative steps.

6.

When doubting in shadows
remember
first buds —

blue Johnny-jump-ups,
white fawn lilies,
pink Chinese hellebore,
crepe-paper Oriental poppy.

Under last year's leaves,
white, bell-shaped
snowdrops uncurl,
first and foremost.

What comes, goes —

but memory, ah, memory
curls out of itself.

7.

Memory comes,
and unfortunately,
goes
when needed most.
Age removes it,
giving instead forgetfulness,

Why can't memory be
a buttercup
we held to our chins
when we were children
to see who liked butter?

This Buttercup Memory
would show
who remembers
what is necessary
and forgets
what needs forgiving.

8.

This is for my mother,
heading into Alzheimer's
like it was a destination,
a one-way, no exit strategy,
all the others
hopelessly lost,
as everything disappears,
nothing remaining.

I might be coming your way.

9.

Until then,
I grab onto fistfuls of light,
keep them in a drawer,
write flames of memory,
turn darkness into origami,
my chin yellow
from holding a buttercup.

The opposite of loss is finding.

Evening Shower at Atake and the Great Bridge

Based on the picture by Utagawa Hiroshige

What we feel is not rain.
Weather will clear and return
with rice, or crabs, or plum tree blossoms
before rain loses its sway.
Evening will be here and gone
before the rooster knows it.

We just about begin when we end.
Rain falls upon us regardless
if we try to shelter ourselves or not.

A lake does not have to be immense
to absorb all this rain,
but it cannot contain all the rain
if it is endlessly filling.

A haiku is simply a prayer. A warbler
knows more about appreciating the day
than I ever will.

Birds fly in to the sky, disappear,
reappearing elsewhere.

The Door

For no known reason there was a door in the field,
free-standing and locked. I know; I tested it.

I do not know which was stranger: a secure door
without walls, or me trying the doorknob.

I walked all around the door,
trying to determine why it was locked.

Perhaps, the door knew
the world was a dangerous place.

I suspect if I found a key, it might be the wrong key.
Or if I unlocked the door, I might find a void.

Some mysteries are determined to remain unknown.

The World Should Be Disturbed

The world should be disturbed — wanting to climb
into cherry blossoms when it snows pink —

proclaiming loudly in the throes of love,
a plaintive call from clouds.

The world should be full of noise,
shaking sleeves of night-shivers,

making a calligraphy of love
out of nothing.

Somewhere,
a thrush shares its four-notes to no one in particular.

In this constant making,
the hibiscus moon is in a flock of star-swans.

A Room Everyone Enters

There is a place without light,
a restless place.
Not one object is still —

a place wanting to touch us,
coloring our cheeks,
making us determined to stay;

a place wanting us to be content,
ready to betray us,
playing soft, romantic music.

The language it speaks is seductive,
making us feel desired,
measured to assure certain results.

I know this room. I see everyone
drawn to this place, hypnotized,
although burned by coming too close.

Acknowledgments

I would like to thank the following journals in which the following poems first appeared, many in slightly different versions or with different titles:

Ayris: "Lifting Out of Ourselves"

Big City Lit: "Before Drawing," "Before Music"

Bigger Stones: "The Letter"

Bolts of Cloth: "In Between"

Identity Crisis: "Before Letters"

The Inflectionist Review: "Nocturne"

Loch Raven Review: "Depleted Uranium"

Moon Magazine: "Walking into Remembrance,"
"Rain is the Face of Desolation," "Is There a Beyond?"

Napalm and Novocain: "Not Seeing Eye-to-Eye"

Nidus: "Before Dance and Drama"

Oddball Magazine: "Not Exactly Sleight-of-Hand"

Poetry Pacific: "Air"

Poppy Road Review: "Glass,"
"There Is a Rawness We Do Not Understand, But Do"

Ragazine: "Entering," "A Red Box," "Silence"

Stone Canoe: "Touch"

Verse-Virtual: "The Door," "The Other,"
"A Room Everyone Enters"

Walnut Literary Review: "Robert Rauschenberg's 'Canyon'"

Wilderness Literary House Review: "What We Do Not Know"

"Before Music" appeared in a special section of *Big City Lit*, comparing it to Wallace Stevens' poem, "The Man with the Blue Guitar"

"Glass Walls Do Not a Barrier Make" was the winner of the *2013 National Broadsided Contest* (theme: Typhoon Haiyan 2013): This contest was to match Joel Haber's artwork.

"Improvisations in Darkness" was a mini-chapbook, *Improvisations in Darkness* (Origami Poetry Project, 2014)

"Nocturne" was nominated for *2017 Orison Anthology* by *The Inflectionist Review*

"Rain is the Face of Desolation" was reprinted *Journeys along the Silk Road Anthology* (Lost Tower Publications, 2015)

"Some Days" appeared in the anthology, *A Roof of Red Tiles & other stories & poems* (Cinnamon Press, Wales, 2014)

"Prelude to Death" appeared in the mini-chapbook, *Dedication* (Origami Poetry Project, 2014)

About the Author

Martin Willitts Jr. is a retired Librarian living in Syracuse, New York. He is a visual artist of Victorian and Chinese paper cutouts. He was nominated for 15 *Pushcart* and 13 *Best of the Net* awards. He provided his hands-on workshop "How to Make Origami Haiku Jumping Frogs" at the *2012 Massachusetts Poetry Festival* and the *2015 Amherst Poetry Festival*.

Winner of the *2012 Big River Poetry Review's William K. Hathaway Award*; *2013 Bill Holm Witness Poetry Contest*; *2013 "Trees" Poetry Contest*; *2014 Broadsided award*; *2014 Dylan Thomas International Poetry Contest*; *Rattle Ekphrastic Challenge, June 2015, Editor's Choice*; *Rattle Ekphrastic Challenge, Artist's Choice, November 2016, Stephen A. DiBiase Poetry Prize*, 2018. He won a *Central New York Individual Artist Award* and provided "Poetry on The Bus" which had 48 poems in local buses including 20 bilingual poems from 7 different languages.

His 23 chapbooks include *"Falling In and Out of Love"* (Pudding House Publications, 2005), *"Lowering Nets of Light"* (Pudding House Publications, 2007), *"The Garden of French Horns"* (Pudding House Publications, 2008), *"Baskets of Tomorrow"* (Flutter Press, 2009), *"The Girl Who Sang Forth Horses"* (Pudding House Publications, 2010), *"Van Gogh's Sunflowers for Cezanne"* (Finishing Line Press, 2010), *"Why Women Are A Ribbon Around A Bomb"* (Last Automat, 2011), *"Protest, Petition, Write, Speak: Matilda Joslyn Gage Poems"* (Matilda Joslyn Gage Foundation, 2011), *"Secrets No One Wants To Talk About"* (Dos Madres Press, 2011), *"How to Find Peace"* (Kattywompus Press, 2012), *"Playing The Pauses In The Absence Of Stars"* (Main Street Rag, 2012), *"No Special Favors"* (Green Fuse Press, 2012), *"The Constellations of Memory and Forgiveness"* (Seven Circles Press, web book, 2014), *"A Is For Aorta"* (Kind of Hurricane Press, e-book, 2014), national chapbook contest winning *"William Blake, Not Blessed Angel But Restless Man"* (Red Ochre Press, 2014), *"Swimming in the Ladle of Stars"* (Kattywompus Press,2014),*"City Of Tents"* (Crisis Chronicles Press, 2014), *"The Way Things Used To Be"* (Writing Knights Press, 2014), *"Late All Night Sessions with Charlie "the Bird" Parker and the Members of Birdland, in Take-Three"* (A Kind Of a Hurricane Press, 2015), *"The Burnt-Over District"* (e-book, Icarus Books, 2015), and *"Martin Willitts Jr Greatest Hits"* (Kattywompus Press, 2016), *Turtle Island Editor's Choice Award* for his chapbook, *"The Wire Fence Holding Back the World"* (Flowstone Press, 2016), *"Nasturtiums in Snow Understand Green Is Coming"* (Foothills Press, 2018), *You Enter, and it All Falls Apart* (Flutter Press, 2019).

His 18 full-length books include *"The Secret Language of the Universe"* (March Street Press, 2006), *"The Hummingbird"* (March Street Press, 2009), *"The Heart Knows, Simply, What It Needs: Poems based on Emily Dickinson, her life and poetry"* (Aldrich Press, 2012), *"Art is an Impression of What an Artist Sees"* (Edgar and Lenore Publishing House, 2013), national ecological award winner for *"Searching for What You Cannot See"* (Hiraeth Press, 2013), *"Before Anything, There Was Mystery"* (Flutter Press, 2014), *"Irises, the Lightning Conductor For Van Gogh's Illness"* (Aldrich Press, 2014), *"God Is Not Amused with What You Are Doing in Her Name"* (Aldrich Press, 2015), *"How to Be Silent"* (FutureCycle Press, 2016), *"Dylan Thomas and the Writer's Shed"* (FutureCycle Press, 2017), *"Three Ages of Women"* (Deerbrook Editions, 2017), *"The Uncertain Lover"* (Dos Madres Press, 2018), *"News from the Slow Country"* (Aldrich Press, 2019), and *"Home Coming Celebration"* (FutureCycle Press, 2019).

Forthcoming books include *"The Unfolding of Love"* (Wipf and Stock Publishers), *"Unexpected"* (Duck Lake Press), and *"Harvest Time"* (Deerbrook Editions)

www.ingramcontent.com/pod-product-compliance
Lightning Source LLC
Chambersburg PA
CBHW032027090426
42741CB00006B/759